LEVEL THREE
(C or Grade 2)

CLASSIC THEMES

BOOK TWO

For PIANO or ELECTRONIC KEYBOARD

Transcribed and Edited by

WESLEY SCHAUM AND JEFF SCHAUM

FOREWORD

This collection is designed as an introduction to classic music by some of the world's greatest composers. Sketches and biographical information about each composer are provided. Although many of the themes may already be familiar, the experience of playing them at piano or keyboard will be satisfying as well as educational.

The music selected is transcribed from well known symphonies, operas, ballets, and orchestral music to widen the student's musical experiences beyond standard piano literature.

INDEX

BALLET THEMES

SYMPHONY THEMES

DESCRIPTIVE THEMES

OPERA THEMES

SCHAUM PUBLICATIONS, INC. 10235 N. Port Washington Road Mequon, WI 53092

07-52
HA-4

SYMPHONY Composers

ANTON DVORAK (DVOR-zhock) *1841-1904*

Dvorak was born in Bohemia, now a part of Czechoslovakia. He is best known as a composer, but also was an organist and viola player. As a teacher at the Prague Conservatory, he attracted students from all over Europe.

This symphony was inspired by Dvorak's visit to the United States where he spent several months living in a Bohemian settlement at Spillville, Iowa. The symphony was written while he was artistic director of the National Conservatory in New York and was first performed by the New York Philharmonic in 1893. Although the *New World Symphony* is his most famous work, he also wrote a large number of piano and chamber music compositions.

CESAR FRANCK (FRAHNK) *1822-1890*

Franck was born in Belgium, but spent most of his life in France. As a student at the Paris Conservatory, he won many awards for organ playing. He later became professor of organ at the Conservatory and organist-choirmaster at the Church of St. Clotilde in Paris. His organ music is still regularly performed in church services and recitals in the United States. He is also known for his chamber music and choral works.

Franck wrote only one symphony. At its premiere in 1888, the musicians did not want to perform it because they thought it was a poor piece of music. The first audience found it difficult to understand and reacted negatively. It is, however, popular with modern audiences and ranks among the greatest symphonies ever written. It is probably Franck's best known work.

ROBERT SCHUMANN (SHOO-mahn) *1810-1856*

Schumann was a German composer and pianist. His wife, Clara, was also a concert pianist. Schumann was the outspoken editor of a music magazine that was very influential in promoting the romantic style of music. He and his wife were close friends of Brahms and were acquainted with many other outstanding composers and performers of the day. Schumann is best known for his piano works and four symphonies.

The premiere of the Fourth Symphony in 1841 was a flop; both critics and audiences disliked it. Ten years later, Schumann was inspired to revise the symphony to its present form. The third movement is a scherzo, a brisk dance-like piece with extended thematic development.

PETER TCHAIKOWSKY (chy-CUFF-skee) *1840-1893*

Tchaikowky was an outstanding Russian composer whose works remain as some of the most popular in the entire musical repertoire. His renowned ballets include *The Nutcracker*, *Swan Lake*, and *Sleeping Beauty*. His piano concertos, violin concerto, and symphonies are frequently performed by orchestras all over the world. Tchaikowsky was the guest of honor at the opening of Carnegie Hall in New York City in 1891. At that time he conducted concerts of his own music in New York, Philadelphia, and Baltimore.

Tchaikowsky wrote a total of six symphonies. The 4th Symphony was written in 1877, and the 5th Symphony in 1888, during a time of patronage by Madame von Meck, a noblewoman who generously supported Tchaikowsky for thirteen years by paying his living expenses. During this time he produced some of his best works. Although the two corresponded regularly, they never met.

DVORAK: *Symphony No. 9, "New World"*

(Theme from Second Movement)

TCHAIKOWSKY: *Symphony No. 4*

(Theme from Second Movement)

TCHAIKOWSKY: *Symphony No. 5*

(Theme from Second Movement)

FRANCK: *Symphony in D minor*

(Theme from First Movement)

SCHUMANN: *Symphony No. 4*

(Theme from Third Movement)

OPERA Composers and Stories

CHARLES GOUNOD (GOO-noe) *1818-1893*

Gounod was born in France. As a student at the Paris Conservatory, he won two prizes for the cantatas he composed. Gounod was very interested in organ composition and church music. He wrote 12 operas, as well as choral and orchestral music. *Faust* was first performed in Paris in 1859.

STORY OF *FAUST*

Faust, an old man, sells his soul to the devil to regain youth and good looks. The new Faust courts Margurite and they have a baby. Margurite's brother, Valentine, returns from a victorious military campaign singing the *Soldiers Chorus.* He is angry when he finds out about Margurite and attempts to kill Faust. The devil intervenes and kills Valentine. Margurite eventually recognizes the devil in Faust. She dies and ascends to heaven while Faust is reclaimed by the devil.

RUGGIERO LEONCAVALLO (lay-on-kah-VAL-loh) *1858-1919*

Leoncavallo was an Italian composer and pianist. As a young man he earned a living playing piano in cafes throughout Europe. Although he wrote songs, piano solos, choral music, and eleven other operas, he is remembered mainly for the opera, *Pagliacci,* which was first performed in 1892.

STORY OF *PAGLIACCI*

Pagliacci (meaning comedy players) is about the loves and intrigues in a small group of actors. Canio, head of the group, jealously watches his wife, Nedda. She refuses to reveal the identity of her lover, Silvio. On stage, Canio must act the part of a clown while inwardly overcome with anger and grief over his wife. During a performance, Silvio attempts to help Nedda, but both are killed by Canio.

WOLFGANG AMADEUS MOZART (MOE-tsart) *1756-1791*

Mozart was born in Salzburg, Austria. He was an extremely gifted child, starting music study at age three, composing by age five, and touring Europe as a performer with his family at age six. Although he died at age 35, he composed a huge amount of instrumental and vocal solo works, chamber music, oratorios, symphonies, sacred music, and 16 operas. He is recognized world wide as one of the greatest musical geniuses of all time. The *Marriage of Figaro* was first performed in 1786, *Don Giovanni* in 1787.

STORY OF *DON GIOVANNI*

Don Giovanni has several romantic pursuits, leaving enemies along the way. The angry father (Commandant) of one of the girls challenges Giovanni to a duel and the Commandant is killed. Giovanni is haunted by the ghost of the Commandant's statue. When Giovanni fails to repent, he is cast into hell.

STORY OF *MARRIAGE OF FIGARO*

This story is from the same source as *Barber of Seville* by Rossini. The events follow after those in *Barber of Seville.* Count Almaviva is flirting with Suzanna, his wife's maid. Figaro, now the count's valet, loves Suzanna but is blocked by Bartolo, a lawyer who has an old marriage contract for Figaro with Marcellina. The count's wife and Suzanna dress as each other to set things straight. All ends well with a double wedding of Figaro/Suzanna and Bartolo/Marcellina.

GIOACCHINO ROSSINI (row-ZEE-nee) *1792-1868*

Rossini was born into an Italian musical family. His father was a trumpet player and his mother a singer. Between 1810 and 1829 he wrote 39 operas which were so successful financially that he composed no others before he died almost 40 years later. *Barber of Seville* was written in 1816. Rossini wrote the entire opera in thirteen days.

STORY OF *BARBER OF SEVILLE*

Count Almaviva seeks the help of Figaro, a barber and jack-of-all-trades, to win the love of the beautiful Rosina. Rosina's greedy guardian, Bartolo, wants Rosina and her money for himself. Figaro and the count disguise themselves in several episodes to deceive Bartolo and woo Rosina. In the end, Rosina weds the count and Bartolo gets her money. *Largo al Factotum* is sung by Figaro, describing his carefree life.

ROSSINI: *Barber of Seville*

("Largo al Factotum della citta" from Act I, Scene 1)

MOZART: *Don Giovanni*

("La ci darem la mano" from Act I, Scene 3)

MOZART: *Marriage of Figaro*

("Non piu andrai" from Act I)

LEONCAVALLO: *Pagliacci*

("Vesti la Giubba" from Act I)

GOUNOD: Faust

("Soldier's Chorus" from Act IV)

BALLET Composers and Stories

ADOLPHE ADAM (ah-DAHN) *1803-1856*

Adam was a French composer of comic operas and ballets which were internationally famous in their day. He was professor of composition at the Paris Conservatory. He wrote 15 ballets, 70 operas, plus sacred music, vocal, and choral pieces. Of his works, only *Giselle* remains in the ballet repertoire. He is also the composer of the well known Christmas song, *O Holy Night*.

STORY OF *GISELLE*

A noble count who is in love with a peasant girl, Giselle, disguises himself as a peasant to win her love. Shortly before their wedding, Giselle finds that she has been deceived and is so upset that she dances herself into a frenzy and dies. Her spirit joins a heavenly group of "Wilis" — other brides who have died before their wedding day. When the count visits Giselle's grave, the Wilis take revenge and he is killed.

JACQUES OFFENBACH (AH-fen-bahk) *1819-1880*

Offenbach was born in Germany, but spent nearly all of his life in France and is, therefore, generally considered a French composer. He was a professional cello player and conducter in Paris. He is most famous for his comic operettas, and wrote 97 of them during his lifetime. He also wrote ballets, vocal music, and cello music.

STORY OF *GAITE PARISIENNE*

"Gaite Parisienne" is a ballet using music selected from various operettas of Offenbach. It reflects life in Paris in the 1860's. This excerpt is popularly known as the "Can-Can," a vigorous high-kicking dance considered naughty and daring in its day because women flounced their skirts revealing their legs.

AMILCARE PONCHIELLI (pahn-kee-ELL-lee) *1834-1886*

Ponchielli was an Italian composer who wrote sacred music, twelve operas, and numerous ballets. Unfortunately, many of his ballets have been lost and only three are known. He is best remembered as the composer of the opera, *La Giocanda*, which includes the *Dance of the Hours*. Ponchielli later took *Dance of the Hours* and made it into a separate ballet piece.

STORY OF *DANCE OF THE HOURS*

The lovely Giocanda spurns the love of Grimaldo, a spy for the inquisition. As revenge, Grimaldo falsely accuses Giocanda's mother. An entangled love affair involving the inquisitor's wife, Laura, and Enzo, whom Giocanda loves, is resolved with the rescue of the mother, the escape of Laura and Enzo and the suicide of Giocanda to avoid Grimaldo. The Dance of the Hours symbolizing dawn, day, evening, and night represents the ultimate triumph of good over evil.

FRANZ SCHUBERT (SHOO-burt) *1797-1828*

Schubert was born in Vienna, Austria. At age 8 he started learning violin from his father. He wrote his first symphony at age 16 and his first Mass at age 17. He had a great gift for composing beautiful melodies and ingenious, imaginative accompaniments. During his lifetime he wrote eight symphonies, three operas, and over six hundred songs for voice and piano.

STORY OF *ROSAMUNDE*

Rosamunde, a beautiful princess, refuses to marry the evil ruler of Cypress who, out of spite, plans to kill her with a poisoned letter. A handsome prince, who is sent to deliver the letter, is in love with Rosamunde. The prince warns Rosamunde, switches letters, and the evil ruler is poisoned by his own letter. Rosamunde and the prince are married.

ADAM: *Giselle*

("Pas de Deux" from Act II)

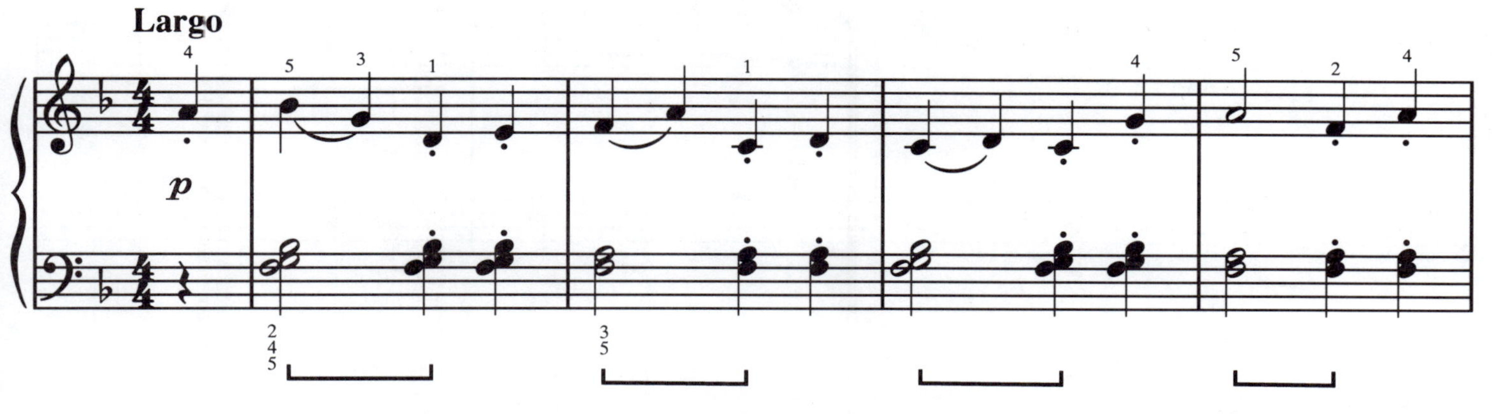

OFFENBACH: *Gaite Parisienne*

("Can Can" from operetta "La Vie Parisienne")

SCHUBERT: *Rosamunde*

(from Act II)

PONCHIELLI: *Dance of the Hours*

(Ballet music from the Opera "La Giocanda")

FELIX MENDELSSOHN (MEN-dell-sohn) *1809-1847*

Mendelssohn was a German-Jewish prodigy who played violin and piano and studied several foreign languages as a child. He started composing as a teenager — the *Midsummer Night's Dream* music was written at age 17. By age 22 he had written a violin concerto and two piano concertos. The quality of these early works is amazingly good. During his lifetime he was famous as a composer, concert pianist, and conductor. He is also credited with research that led to the revival of interest in the music of J.S. Bach.

STORY OF *MIDSUMMER NIGHT'S DREAM*

This music was written to be played between acts of the Shakespeare play, *Midsummer Night's Dream,* and relates to the story as it progresses. The *Nocturne,* meaning "night piece," was planned between the third and fourth acts of the play. The famous wedding march ("Here Comes the Bride") is from this same work.

CAMILLE SAINT-SAENS (sann-SAWN) *1835-1921*

Saint-Saens, born in France, was a very gifted child who gave a formal debut recital at age 10, by which time he had memorized all 32 of Beethoven's piano sonatas. After graduating from the Paris Conservatory, he became famous as a virtuoso organist and master of improvisation. He was the first well-known composer to write music for a movie in 1908. He appeared in the United States in 1915 as a guest conductor.

STORY OF *THE SWAN*

The flowing melody of *The Swan* represents the smooth gliding of a swan swimming on a calm lake. It is part of a suite for orchestra called *Carnival of the Animals,* in which various animals are portrayed in a whimsical, humorous style. Saint-Saens regarded it as frivolous. He was so sensitive about his reputation as a serious composer that he forbade performance or publication of *Carnival of the Animals* during his lifetime.

JEAN SIBELIUS (seh-BAY-lee-us) *1865-1957*

Sibelius is Finland's best known composer. His activities as composer and teacher were so highly regarded in his homeland that he was granted a ten year income by the Finnish government. He wrote chamber music, vocal music, operas, seven symphonies, and other orchestral music. One of his most famous compositions, *Finlandia,* reflected his deep love for his native land.

STORY OF *VALSE TRISTE*

This music was written for a play titled, *Kuolema,* meaning "Death." A woman, delirious with a terminal illness, rises from her bed to engage in a ghostly dance with the spirits of death. In a final burst of effort, the pace of the dance becomes more agitated until the woman falls exhausted on the threshold of death.

JOHANN STRAUSS, JR. (STROWS) *1825-1899*

Strauss, known as the "Waltz King" because of about 400 waltzes written during his lifetime, was born in Austria. His father and brothers, Josef and Eduard, were also composers of waltzes and all conducted their own dance bands. The waltz was a new dance at the time, extremely popular and considered avant garde and somewhat daring because the couples held each other while dancing. Elaborate ballrooms were frequently crowded with patrons. The waltz personified the elegance of upper-class Viennese social life.

STORY OF *TALES FROM THE VIENNA WOODS*

During this time, Vienna, the capital of Austria, was the center of European culture and music. *Tales from the Vienna Woods* was originally written for orchestra. Along with many of Strauss' waltzes, it musically portrays the sophistication and vitality of Vienna.

SAINT-SAENS: *The Swan*

(from "Carnival of the Animals")

STRAUSS: *Tales From the Vienna Woods*

(Op. 325, for orchestra)

SIBELIUS: *Valse Triste*

(from music for "Kuolema", Op. 44)

MENDELSSOHN: *Nocturne*

(from "Midsummer Night's Dream")

THEMES by the MASTERS ... Every Student Should Know

All Titles — LEVEL FOUR

- Music Selected for its EFFECTIVENESS in TEACHING
- Each Book Includes BIOGRAPHICAL DATA and COMPOSER PORTRAIT
- Collections Include Themes from SYMPHONIES, CHAMBER MUSIC, VOCAL LITERATURE, OPERA and PIANO

BEST OF BACH

INCLUDES: Air for G String — Bouree
Gavotte — Jesu, Joy of Man's Desiring
March in D Major — Minuet in G Major
Minuet in G Minor — Musette
My Heart Ever Faithful — Siciliano

BEST OF BEETHOVEN

INCLUDES: Andante from 5th Symphony
Bagatelle — Ecossaise — Fur Elise
Heavens Declare His Glory
Minuet from Sonata Op.49, No.2
Minuet in G — Moonlight Sonata

BEST OF MOZART

INCLUDES: Air in C (Marriage of Figaro)
Allegro in B-flat, K3 — Lullaby
Hand in Hand (Don Giovanni)
Minuet (Symphony in E-flat)
Overture (Marriage of Figaro)

Excerpt from "BEST OF BEETHOVEN"

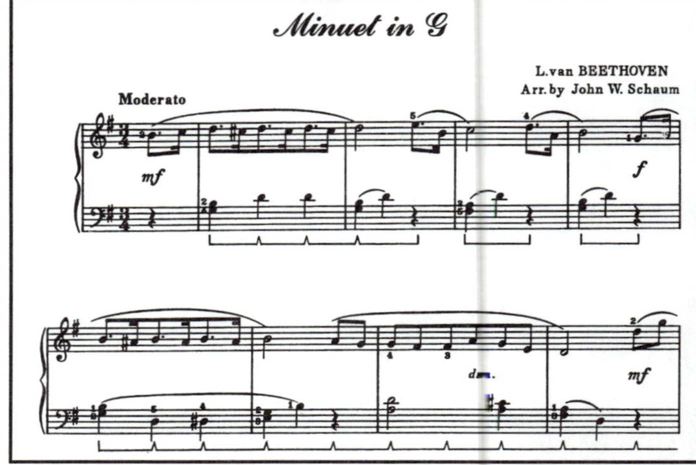

BEST OF SCHUBERT

CONTENTS:

- Cradle Song
- Hark, Hark, the Lark
- Impromptu, Op.142, No.2
- Love Theme (from "Unfinished Symphony")
- March Militaire
- Minuet from Sonata, Op.78
- Moment Musical, Op.94, No.3
- Rosamunde Ballet Music, Op.26
- Serenade
- Sweet Repose (Du bist die Ruh')
- Theme from Octet, Op.166
- Trout
- Valses Nobles, Op.77
- Waltz in C

BEST OF TCHAIKOWSKY

CONTENTS:

- Chanson Triste
- Eugene Onegin Waltz
- Italian Caprice
- March Slav
- None But the Lonely Heart
- Piano Concerto Theme
- Romance
- Romeo and Juliet Love Theme
- Serenade for Strings
- Sleeping Beauty Waltz
- Song Without Words
- Swan Lake Finale
- Sweet Dreams
- Waltz from Swan Lake